Linda,
you can
declutter!
Deb Cabral
10/29/13

DeClutter Your Life NOW!
A motivational guide to tackle
the clutter in ALL aspects of your life

By Deborah J. Cabral
"The DeClutter Coach"

DeClutter Your Life NOW!
A motivational guide to tackle the clutter
in ALL aspects of you life

Contact Information:
46 Genesee Street
New Hartford, NY 13413
deb@decluttercoachdeb.com

Queens Island Publishing
Utica, New York
2012

ISBN-13: 978-0-615-66393-7

Edited by Kate Ferguson
Designed by Michelle Truett, 484 Design, Inc.
Cover photography by Nancy L. Ford Photography
Make-up by Brittany Miller, Runway Hair Salon
New Hartford, NY
Owner - Kelly Rae Dziuban

All stories written in this book are true, although some names have been changed.

To my family – Dan, Shannon, Tom and Carly.
I love you with all my heart!

Table of Contents

Preface

For as long as I can remember, I've been passionate about motivating people to make positive changes in their lives. As a young teen, I began volunteering and learned early on how helping others can ultimately help yourself feel happier and more fulfilled.

In addition to my love of helping people, I have always loved organizing. I know how difficult it can be to juggle multiple tasks and roles, and how easy it is to become disorganized not only in the physical sense, but mentally as well. As a wife, mother of three and active community member, I've had to learn to balance the many demands of family, work, and giving back to the community.

I began my career in the corporate world over two decades ago. For part of my career, I was responsible for improving workflow systems, providing training, and motivating workers to be more productive at their jobs. In addition to streamlining work units and supervising business analysts, I helped develop systems to aid people in doing their jobs more efficiently.

Then everything changed. In 2002, I was involved in a serious car accident that altered the course of my life forever. After a difficult series of surgeries and years of rehab, I began to feel healthier and was motivated to realize my longtime dream of combining my two passions: organizing and helping people. My first business, The DeClutter Coach, was born! Over the next two years, growing demand led to the rapid expansion of my business to include DC Efficiency Consulting, our corporate division; "Organization Motivation!," our hit television show, and "Organized in :60 Seconds," news segments that air in Central New York with plans to expand nationwide.

Today, I am fortunate to be able to work with busy corporations and families to help them manage their time and tasks more efficiently for improved productivity and to bring harmony into their lives. I've met so many amazing people and have been inspired by the changes they have made. Many have been complete transformations.

This book is a compilation of the many ideas I've shared with my clients. In addition to my tried-and-true tips and techniques for organizing yourself and all aspects of your life, you'll find an abundance of amazing success stories, helpful self-reflection quizzes, and words of wisdom that I've come to live by. I want you to know that you CAN make positive changes in your life, and I hope this book will motivate you to do just that!

- Deborah J. Cabral, New Hartford, NY, August 2012

Acknowledgements

There are so many important people to thank whose love, guidance, assistance and support made this book possible. I am extremely grateful to:

My amazing husband, Dan, who is the most organized man I know and my true partner in managing our household. He did more than his share at home so I could write this book and supported me every step of the way!

Our children Shannon, Tom and Carly who inspire me everyday to be the best mom I can be!

My Mom (the original DeClutter Coach as she calls herself) and Dad who passed on the "organizing gene" and taught me the importance of hard work, dedication and making a daily To Do list.

To my sisters Janine and Stacey for making my job as a big sister an easy one.

To my talented team Mary Carole Griffin (my friend and co-star on Organization Motivation! and Organized in 60 Seconds), Michelle McCarrick Truett (the best graphic designer in the world!) Matt Ossowski, Charles Thompson, Collette Aurand, Stacey Lanpher and Sue Kraft. I could not do what I do without all of you. You are awesome, dedicated and make every day fun! Special thanks to Michelle for designing this book and having patience with my "revisions" and to Mary Carole for proofreading.

To Patti Jweid and Barb Nicolette who for the past 15 years have been the most supportive "ya ya sisters" and have always been there for me in good times and bad!

To Mary Malone McCarthy and Ivy Slater - the best business coaches ever. Thanks for believing in me.

To the advertisers of our show, Organization Motivation! especially my friends at JAY-K Lumber and Mohawk Valley Community College, our founding sponsors, who took a chance on my crazy idea!

To the amazing women who helped me with my business - Sharon St. John and Roxanne Mutchler at the Small Business Development Center, and Dr. Pat Laino, Donna Rebisz and Tricia Badgley at the Women's Business Center. Your guidance has been instrumental in the success of my business.

To Kate Ferguson for an amazing job editing this book.

To my clients who allowed me to use their before and after photos and testimonials in this book. You are the reason I love what I do!

DeClutter Your Life NOW!
A motivational guide to tackle
the clutter in ALL aspects of your life

By Deborah J. Cabral
"The DeClutter Coach"

CHAPTER 1

What is Clutter?

Clutter. When you hear the word, I bet you probably think of "stuff." But this isn't just a book about "stuff," because clutter is about a whole lot more than that.

When we think of clutter, most people immediately think of physical clutter - the pile of unopened mail on the kitchen table or the unfolded clean clothes still in the laundry basket. But clutter can also take the form of things we can't see. There's mental or emotional clutter, or what I refer to as "life clutter." This type of clutter, which I'll discuss in depth in the next chapter, can include relationship stress, anxiety surrounding your job, or unspoken fears that you carry with you.

Some people have financial clutter, which leads to poor money management, worrying about bills, and a whole other set of frustrations or anxieties. More on that in Chapter 5.

And then there's the actual clutter you see in your house every day, that "stuff" you've been thinking of. We never seem to have enough space for it! Did you know that in the last 30 years, the size of the average American home has grown nearly 53 percent? The houses we're living in today are much larger than what our grandparents occupied. And yet, the number of long-term storage facilities in our country continues to rise. Today there are more than 35,000 nationwide!

Do you own clutter, or does your clutter own you? Sure, it's natural to want more things and to hold onto them. Our ancestors had to save everything that might be useful -- their mere survival depended on it. But times have changed, and the things we hold onto now don't always help us. Quite the opposite, in fact. Not only does clutter steal our space, it jeopardizes our relationships and monopolizes our time. Clutter can even affect our health.

Health Risks Associated with Clutter

Your outer world is a reflection of your inner world!

Physical clutter in your home and your work space can breed mental and emotional clutter. This disorganization in your environment drains your energy and causes anxiety and stress. It puts your body in a state of chaos. While the body is in this state, it is nearly impossible to function properly, think clearly and be productive. When your body is stressed, it is difficult to make important life choices such as exercising regularly, eating properly and caring for your home. By bringing order back into your living and working spaces, your mind is calmed and therefore able to think more clearly. This order makes living a healthier life much easier to attain.

Research has shown that Americans as a whole waste nine million hours per day searching for misplaced items, such as keys, money, shoes, tools, etc. In addition, 23 percent of adults say they pay bills late, with penalties, because they have lost them.

Types of Clutter

- Physical Clutter
- Mental/Emotional Clutter or "Life Clutter"
- Financial Clutter

Effects of Clutter on Health

- Stress: over the long term, even low levels of stress can affect your health
- Depression: feelings of guilt or helplessness
- Chronic pain and fatigue
- Anxiety, anger, frustration, irritability and emotional issues: "I don't want to live like this!"
- Feeling overwhelmed, difficulty concentrating, sleep issues
- Asthma, wheezing, chronic cough, chest tightness or other diseases resulting from poor air quality from dust
- Fire & tripping hazards

Clutter and Weight

Did you know that clutter is even linked to weight gain? Studies have shown that people who seek to lose weight often occupy cluttered spaces, or carry some type of "emotional clutter," which I'll discuss in the next chapter. Many possess a combination of the two.

Weight gain and obesity are a definite health concern today. In fact, the Centers for Disease Control estimates that the numbers have risen dramatically over the last 20 years, and more than one-third of U.S. adults (35.7%) and approximately 17% of children and adolescents aged 2-19 years are obese today. Obesity-related illnesses such as heart disease, stroke, type 2 diabetes, and even certain types of cancer are also on the rise.

If you are trying to lose weight, take a look around your home, and think about how the space you occupy is contributing to healthy or unhealthy eating habits. What's your kitchen like? A cluttered kitchen is a place where you do not want to spend any time. You enter quickly and grab processed, unhealthy foods to eat and do not have any place to cook a meal. To the contrary, a clean, decluttered kitchen is a place where you will make healthy eating choices and be motivated to prepare healthy meals.

To declutter and become healthy, you need to change habits and behaviors. Remember, it takes 21 days to form a new habit, so persistence is key!

For many families, all it takes is setting up a system of organization, establishing routines, and planning for success. These are simple steps, but they're sure to have an enormous impact on your physical and mental well-being (For more on this, see Chapter 4!).

Other Health Issues

Whether you realize it or not, there are some who love a cluttered environment -- rodents. Insects. Dust mites. Cockroaches. For these unwelcome visitors, your cluttered room is a dream home! In addition, the moisture brought on by excess clutter causes mold, fungus and germs resulting in allergies and other respiratory issues.

Most people have clutter in some form in their homes. But for some, the clutter can become so extreme that it affects the person's quality of life. This is compulsive hoarding. Currently, about 1.5 million people suffer from compulsive hoarding, living in homes where clutter has overtaken every room of the house. For compulsive hoarders, it is impossible and even emotionally painful to get rid of their possessions.

Compulsive hoarders require the help of a therapist or counselor to help change their habits and behaviors. If you or someone you know is a compulsive hoarder, know that there is no shame in this disorder. It is anxiety based and usually occurs after a traumatic event. People seek help, get better and overcome hoarding, but it cannot be done alone.

Life Clutter

I always say, "Physical clutter breeds mental clutter." Many of our clients that struggle with clutter also experience "life clutter" (more on this in Chapter 2!) Life clutter can come in many forms, from unhealthy relationships to negative beliefs about ourselves. It affects our energy, our thoughts, our self-esteem, and our spirits. Just like a cluttered physical environment can prevent us from thinking clearly or being productive, this emotional clutter can

Take small steps EVERY day to declutter, one area at a time. Small changes consistently over time yield BIG results!

make us feel frustrated, angry, scared, or simply lost.

Life clutter makes us forget what is really important, and stops us from living in the present. It denies us peace of mind. It has the potential to take over our homes and our lives. Many of our clients who have "life clutter" say they feel overwhelmed -- busy everyday, but not very productive. They'll tell us, "I have been going all day long, but I never feel a sense of accomplishment." Sound familiar? I am sure many of us can relate to that feeling on certain days.

Clutter means different things to different people

But it doesn't have to be that way! Organizing yourself and your life takes time, effort, and dedication -- but you CAN do it! Before we can deal with the clutter in any aspect of our lives, it's important to think about why we're holding on to it.

Excuses that Hold Us Back from Removing the Clutter From Our Lives

1. I might need it someday.
2. This isn't clutter; it's a collection.
3. I've had this since I was a child.
4. It was given to me, and I'd feel guilty if I got rid of it.
5. I can't pass up a sale; look at all the money I'm saving!

I've worked with hundreds of people over the years, and I've seen and heard every form of the excuses above, and many more. But these excuses don't help when it comes to making tangible, lasting changes. If you'd like to see results but insist on maintaining the same old patterns, realize it's not going to work. It's time to stop sabotaging yourself! You need to be willing to make changes, create new habits, and learn new systems that will help you move forward. It IS possible to overcome your fears, anxieties, and any other obstacles that have been holding you back.

You can do it! If you've picked up this book, it means that you're interested in finding out how decluttering can help you or someone you care about.

I would love to be able to work with each and every one of you, one-on-one in your homes, offices, or wherever you have clutter. But I can't. So in the following chapters, I am going to show you how to stop procrastinating, forget about making excuses, and just get started!

It's time to take action! It's time to FINALLY get organized -- and STAY that way!

Now, are you with me? Then let's go!

CHAPTER 2

Managing Life Clutter

One of my favorite quotes is from *Life's Greatest Lessons: 20 Things That Matter* by Hal Urban (Simon & Schuster 2003): "Life is simpler when we know what is essential."

I didn't give this idea much thought until a car accident ten years ago changed the course of my life forever. There's nothing like being seriously injured to put things in perspective and make you realize what's really important: family, friends and the power of keeping a positive frame of mind at all times.

After many surgeries and years of painful rehab, I finally began to feel healthier and decided it was time to go after my life-long dream of starting my own business. By combining my two passions - helping people and organizing, I started my business - The DeClutter Coach. It has shown me how it's absolutely essential to simplify your life and focus on the positive each day.

Think about what's __really__ important

In our busy, over-scheduled lives, sometimes we forget what is truly important and simply "go through the motions" each day, until we pass out at bedtime from exhaustion. While you may not be able to see its effects as easily as you can see physical clutter, the "life clutter" you carry with you can be mentally and emotionally draining.

In order to conquer the strain of life clutter, it's important to take a few steps back, let go, and reassess what's important. Remember some of the greatest gains we make often start with small steps. If you are looking for ways to see the calm through the chaos, here are some ideas to implement right now.

How to Conquer Life Clutter

1   Slow Down! Every minute of every day does not need to be filed with things to do, places to go or people to see. Take time to rest and clear your mind.

2   Keep your commitments (both personal and professional) to only those things you are truly passionate about. Consider eliminating one current volunteer commitment from your life that does not bring you a sense of fulfillment. You do not need to be everything to everyone!

3   Start a new hobby or resurrect a hobby you really enjoyed but haven't done in a while because there is "not enough time". Make the time for fun and enjoyment - you deserve it!

The "life clutter" you carry with you can be mentally and emotionally draining.

4   Use a daily planner. When you write down your schedule every day, it is easy to start to see time as "tangible." Schedule downtime for you and your family to laugh and enjoy each other's company.

5   Learn to politely say NO! How many times have you agreed to do something that you really did not want to do out of guilt? Let go of the guilt and give yourself permission to decline a request or invitation that does not fit into your schedule or passions.

Change is never easy, but is a necessity when we are feeling overwhelmed with life's responsibilities and challenges. To be content, we need to have some balance in our lives.

Here's what some of my clients have said after dealing with their own "life clutter:"

"Deb shared her expertise with our Go Red for Women Team on How to Declutter for a Healthy Life. It is amazing how clutter can affect so many aspects of our lives, including our overall health. There was an overwhelming response to her informative, inspiring, and motivational presentation. Many said they were starting today and scheduling 15 minutes to start decluttering their space."

Marguerite L.,
Community and Regional Affairs Manager,
Excellus BlueCross BlueShield

"Deb recently came to speak to a group of our employees about 'DeCluttering for a Healthy Life.' She offered fantastic advice and applied practical solutions to incorporate into our everyday lives at home and at work. Employees walked away feeling inspired and motivated to make changes to their current habits and identified ways they can avoid the unnecessary stress of being disorganized. Thank you Deb!"

Lori N.,
Human Resources Manager
First Source Federal Credit Union

Achieving perfect balance every day is unrealistic, but we can manage our life so there is more calm and peace. The benefits will be instantaneous. Give it a try!

More Ways to Organize Yourself and Prevent "Life Clutter"
- Look your best. When you look good, you feel good.
- Schedule "me" time everyday!
- Cultivate your friendships.
- Love your spouse/significant other and cultivate that relationship everyday.
- Love your children with all your heart. And remember it is healthy for them to see that you have a life other than being their parent.

Relationships
Strong, positive relationships with family and friends are the foundation for a happy and healthy emotional life. But in our busy lives, we often neglect the ones we care about most. Here are some ways to help foster healthy relationships with your loved ones.

Your Spouse
- Decide how and when you will communicate.
- Establish relationship guidelines.
- Establish goals - personal, professional and financial.
- Agree to disagree when necessary. Someone does not always have to be right.
- Create a plan to share chores and parenting responsibilities.
- Support each other in good times, and the bad times will be easier to handle.

Your Family
- Laugh and have fun with each other, every day.
- Schedule down time to just be together, without planned activities.
- Practice your faith and make it an important part of your family life.
- Have regular family meetings where family members can discuss any issues they may have.
- Make family dinner time sacred: no phones, no TV, no distractions.
- Support each other's passions and encourage each other's dreams.

Your Friends
- Make time to communicate with your friends, whether it's in person, on the phone, or via e-mail.

- Schedule regular get-togethers, whether it's weekly, monthly, or a few times a year.
- Remind yourself that strong social relationships are not only beneficial, they're essential!

Tried and True Tactics for Removing Life Clutter

Regardless of the size of your family or the situations in your household, it's always important to take a step back and evaluate the "life clutter" that is draining you mentally and emotionally. We may not be able to see it, but its effects are there, and can possibly be even more damaging than the physical clutter in our homes. The following pieces of advice from Hal Urban's book *Life's Greatest Lessons, 20 Things That Matter Most* (Simon & Schuster, 2003) have served me well over the years, and I hope they'll remind you to stay on track, keep focused, and be positive!

- Maintain a positive outlook regardless of the situation.
- Be strong when you are faced with difficulties and challenges.
- Show your family and friends that you love them. Tell them too.
- Strive to bring out the best in people, even yourself.
- Have a good attitude, even when things are tough.
- Live your life with integrity.
- Show kindness to others.
- Respect yourself and others.
- Laugh and have fun every day.
- Be fair and honest in everything you do.
- Work hard and never give up.
- Be thankful.
- Avoid being judgmental.

CHAPTER 3

Organizing Your Family

Imagine the scene: It's breakfast time, and you're scrambling to finish getting dressed, get your kids ready for school, make lunches, and feed everyone. The day has barely begun, but you're exhausted. Sound familiar?

There's a better way to start your day! I've helped lots of busy families get organized and find the routines that work best for them. With a little planning, some practice, and lots of follow-through, you'll start each day feeling less-stressed and more energized!

The Family Hub

The Family Hub is a great way to help busy families keep track of everything from activities and appointments to homework assignments and meals. Your hub can be anywhere -- in a kitchen, mudroom, or hallway -- but I suggest you put it somewhere centrally located so that it's easy to access.

Here's what you need to create your Family Hub:

<u>A Family Calendar</u>: Purchase a dry-erase calendar with different colored markers, one for each family member, or use a paper calendar with colored pencils or pens. List the times for after-school activities, meetings, appointments, and even when school projects or library books are due.

<u>Bulletin Board</u>: Use this to display school calendars, sports schedules, lunch menus, phone numbers, and other important information. This will save time by helping you keep everything at a glance.

<u>Folders or Large Clips</u>: Colored-coded folders or binder clips are a great way to keep track of all the paperwork that tends to accumulate with kids. You can even color-code by family member! Keep artwork, papers that need to be signed, party invitations, etc. together. Clean out the folder weekly. When artwork piles up, involve your child in the decision-making process and ask him/her to only keep the top five favorites. Scan or take a photo of some of the others that they liked but did not decide to keep.

<u>Family Meal Binder</u>: As a family, decide on 25 or so "go to" meals that everyone enjoys. Keep the recipes in the binder. Use plastic page protectors to keep them clean while you're cooking. Have family members help with meal prep, cooking and clean up. Periodically weed out recipes that you no longer use. Consider your family's schedule in the planning process. If your child has a baseball game Tuesday night, why not prepare a crock-pot meal? Start it in the morning and it's ready when you  get home. As time permits, cook in bulk and freeze to use on nights when time is limited.

<u>Computerized Grocery List</u>: Create a computerized grocery list for all of your weekly or bi-weekly grocery needs. Organize it by cat-

egory and list all the items you frequently purchase. This should include all the ingredients you need for your 25 "go to" meals. Keep the list handy so that all family members can take part in circling items that need to be purchased on your next shopping trip. For some clients, we even organize the list by aisle based on their preferred grocery store. This makes shopping a breeze! No more dashing off a list on scrap paper and getting home to realize you've forgotten an important ingredient.

Watch me in action as I help one client create a Family Hub! Check out organizationmotivation.com, EPISODE 5, SEGMENT 1, "Family Hub" episode.

Family Chores Chart: Each family member should help in keeping your home clean and running smoothly. When each person takes ownership over a household task, everyone will feel a sense of value and pride in their home. Children as young as three can help with household chores, such as folding towels or putting away their toys. Even teenagers must be made to participate as contributing members of the family. No chores done? No cell phone! Not only will you have a calm and orderly home, you'll be teaching your children to be responsible, as well!

Developing and using a family hub can be life-changing. Just ask my client Tricia, who now has the family hub down to a science.

"As a single Mom raising four children, working full time, and care-taking a home, time is precious. I was utterly frustrated with the piles of shoes in front of the door, the backpacks and coats lying on the floor, and was tired of answering the question, 'Mom where's my.....' DeClutter Coach Deb came into my home and within a few hours crafted a unique plan that keeps my family of five organized. The hub, launch zone, and family scheduling area created a simple, yet effective way for my children to take responsibility for organizing their own coats, shoes, backpacks, school papers, and even created a way for them to keep track of important events on our color coded calendar. Deb's simple organizational plan has create a sense of calm in our home and opened up important conversations about time management, prioritizing, and taking responsibility for how we choose to spend our time. Deb's family centered organizational

plan was brilliantly executed, and easy to follow. My four children, two of whom are disabled, are all able to keep themselves organized!"

Tricia S.
homeowner and working mom of four

When I checked up on Tricia a few weeks after our session, she told me about another added benefit of the family hub: not only were her children keeping themselves more organized, they had begun using the calendar to remind her of important events and times and keep mom on track! Way to go!

Zones

In addition to the family hub, it's helpful to have other designated areas to help routines run smoothly, especially when it comes to school. Areas such as a lunch making zone and a launch/drop zone don't have to be fancy, but when implemented and utilized correctly, you'll be amazed at the results!

<u>Lunch Making Zone</u>: No more running all over the kitchen when it's time to make lunch! Keep everything in one convenient location. Store reusable lunch bags, plastic bags, spoons, forks, snack items, bread, etc. in an easy-to-reach place in your kitchen. After grocery shopping, immediately bag snack items in small snack size bags to make lunch packing a snap! Involve children in the lunch making process to help them foster independence.

<u>Snack Zone</u>: Create a drawer or shelf in your pantry specifically for snacks for your children. These could include healthy munchies such as crackers, pretzels, nuts or granola bars. Store them at eye level so that children can learn to help themselves. Designate one shelf in your refrigerator for healthy snacks for kids, such as grapes, cut-up apples, baby carrots, and hummus. When healthy foods are easily accessible, the entire family will be more likely to eat them. (Of course, there's always room for a few cookies!)

<u>Launch/Drop Zone</u>: This is a convenient place to store book bags, shoes, sneakers, boots, coats, sports bags, and umbrellas. You don't need to have a beautifully designed mudroom to be organized and efficient.

Carve out a small area in your kitchen, entryway, or hallway and set up easily accessible systems to keep your family organized, such as hooks, cubbies, shoe racks, shelves, and baskets. For younger children, install these items at their eye level. This will make getting out the door a breeze!

Homework Zone: Create a mobile homework zone. Use a basket or plastic bin with a handle to store everything your children might need while doing homework, such as looseleaf paper, scissors, rulers, magic markers, pens, pencils, erasers, calculator, etc. Store it in a convenient location, and bring it out at homework time so that children will have what they need at their fingertips. No more, "mom, I need a stapler!" When homework time is over the mobile zone can be put away until the next time.

Mail/Bill Paying Zone: Carve out a small area in your kitchen or family room, or create a mobile mail and bill paying zone. Some families incorporate it right into their family hub! Use a decorative basket or bin and include such items as envelopes, stamps, return address labels, your address book, and letter opener. Keep a folder for bills to be paid. If room permits, an expanding file folder or desk organizer is another great way to organize your mail and bills. It's easy to pay your bills on time when everything you need is in one convenient location. The key to maintaining this area is consistency -- open and handle your mail EVERY DAY!

The Value of Routines

The key to eliminating chaos and creating a peaceful, relaxing atmosphere at home is planning, routine, and consistency. Create a plan and routines that work for your family. Use them consistently so everyone knows what to expect and what is expected of them. Involve all family members in the planning stage so it becomes the family's plan, not just your plan. Fine tune and make adjustments to the plan as needed.

In the mornings: Create a morning routine checklist. Some families find it helpful to decide on a set wake up time or to schedule bathroom time for each family member. A checklist of morning activities such as getting dressed, brushing teeth, and making the bed will also help smaller children participate and start the day with a sense of accomplishment. For older children, it's important for them to begin to handle these tasks on their own with minimal reminders from parents.

In the afternoons: As soon as your children arrive home from school, create a 60 second routine where they take off their shoes, hang their coats and empty their bookbags and lunchbag. As they start to unwind, let them be responsible for getting their own drink and snack from the pantry or refrigerator snack zone. Every family handles homework differently. There's no right or wrong way, as long as there's consistency. Parents should do their "homework" while the kids do theirs. Use this time to sign permission slips, go through school flyers and mark important dates on the calendar, file papers and artwork you are keeping, and discard unnecessary papers. Handle paper as soon as it comes home EVERY DAY to avoid unnecessary clutter!

In the evenings: Create an evening routine to prepare for the next day. Pack book bags and check schedules to determine what is needed (gym clothes, library book, instrument), lay out clothes and all accessories for the next day (including shoes and socks), make lunches, and fill water bottles. You can even set out cereal bowls for the next morning. Have the kids help!

Preparing for Back to School
- Shop early for school supplies. Buy extras.
- Start bedtime routine one week before school starts.
- Start serving breakfast and lunch close to school schedule to adjust your child's appetite.
- Do a first day of school practice run for younger children.
- Clean out your child's closet and drawers; get rid of all clothes that do not fit. It will be easier to choose outfits when the closet is less cluttered. Make a list of items needed before you go clothes shopping.

- Start a lunch money jar with extra singles and change for lunches or find out if your school has a pay ahead plan if your children plan to purchase lunch at school.
- If your children bring lunch, make sure your lunch zone is fully stocked.

The Key to Creating Successful Family Routines

1. Establishing routines that work for your family.
2. Consistency.
3. Tweak systems that aren't working well and re-adjust as necessary.

Helping Your Children Disconnect

Not so long ago, parents didn't have to worry about their children texting or surfing social media sites at all hours of the day and night. But these days, it seems every child is connected to a cell phone or other electronic device -- and these devices are always on!

In fact, one study found that children's media activity, including playing video games, texting friends from their cell phone, surfing online, or reading on an e-reader averages about 6.5 hours a day! And that does not include the time they are in school.

93% of children age 12-17 go online Of those kids, 55% use social media such as Facebook, Twitter or YouTube.

Here are some tips to help your children disconnect and break the addiction to their wired lives.

Power down. Turn off the phone at bedtime. Statistics show many teens (and adults) actually sleep with their phones! They can't sleep well because they are over stimulated and cannot turn off their minds enough to relax and fall asleep.

Set limits. Limit the number of hours your child is allowed to be on social media sites or the Internet -- and stick with it!

Prevent interruptions. Do not allow your children to bring their phones to the dinner table or other family activities.

<u>Remove the temptations</u>. Ask your child to shut off their notifications for text messages, e-mail, Facebook, Twitter, etc.

<u>Set a good example</u>! Remember, actions speak louder than words! Your children are watching you, so be a good role model for them!

Avoid Overscheduling

Just as being tied to electronic devices can be a drain on the mental and emotional lives of you and your children, so can the burden of an over-scheduled family. When we're so busy running from one activity to the next, it's difficult to slow down and appreciate the present. Here are some tips to avoid over-scheduling.

Agree on the ground rules as a family - for example; one sport or activity per season, or limit the commitment to two afternoons or evenings during the week. Schedule things in moderation and only sign up for activities your child really enjoys.

- Know the time required before they sign up. Will it interfere with homework, family life, etc.?

- Try to carpool with other parents for practices to make life easier.

- Balance activities for all the children - and yourself!

- Know when to say no! School work and family time should come first!

<u>Schedule downtime</u>! Downtime is just as important as all of these activities, if not more! Remember to make time to relax and "just be."

Sports

There's nothing better than kids who love being active... except the stress that accompanies a hectic sports schedule. So many sports, so little time, right? With all the different sporting activities your children are involved in, no wonder your garage and mudroom become cluttered and disorganized with all the equipment that accompanies these sports.

But don't panic! Here's one of my favorite tips to ensure you'll be ready for the big game. (For more great ways to get all that sporting equipment in order, see Chapter 4!)

Create Sports Bags

Whatever the sport, your children will need a bag to transport their items to and from games and practices. It's best to have a separate bag for each sport in an easy to access area so they can grab it and go. Make your children responsible for making sure everything they need is in the bag before it's time to leave. This is an important life lesson that will help them learn organizational and time management skills. To give them a head start, make a list of what is needed in each bag. Laminate the list so they can refer to it if necessary.

With a little planning, the days of arriving at your child's game without what they need will be just a fading memory.

Getting Organized for College

Seems like just yesterday you were attending their Little League games, and now it's off to college! As a mom of two college students, I know how important it is to start them off on the right track with organization.

Tips for College Bound Students

For all of my college-bound readers, here are some tips that will help you gear up for success:

<u>Dorm Living</u>: Space is at an ultimate minimum! Bring only essential items with you to school. Use storage units of all shapes and sizes to maximum efficiency. Create an organized workspace for studying. The less you have on your desk the better. A cluttered desk creates a cluttered mind!

<u>Time Management</u>: this is one of the biggest struggles among college freshman. The newfound freedom can easily set you off course. Use a daily planner to record classes, homework assignments, project due dates and campus events. Schedule study time or it won't happen. Scheduling promotes predictability. Predictability promotes productivity!

<u>Finances</u>: Set up a budget and stick to it! Be accountable for your spending. Avoid using credit cards unless you can pay the balance off each month.

<u>Campus Resources</u>: Familiarize yourself with the resources your campus has to offer. You never know when you will need them. Campus resources include: the library, campus security, student counseling, office of residential life and the health center, to name a few. Record the location, phone number and hours of operation of each in your daily planner.

<u>Communicate with your parents on a regular basis</u>! Parents just want to know you are safe, healthy and happy. Stay in touch as often as you can!

Tips for Parents of College Bound Students
Here are some things to keep in mind as your child goes off to school.

<u>Let go</u>: You've done a wonderful job raising them, now the hard part-letting them go! College students adjust much quicker and easier when parents show confidence in their ability to handle themselves. On move in day, help them unpack and say goodbye - quickly!

<u>Know they will make mistakes</u>: It's a part of becoming a responsible adult. Provide guidance, but let your child handle issues that arise on his or her own first before coming in and rescuing them.

<u>Communicate on their terms</u>: Facebook and texting are the prime modes of communication for this generation. If you don't know how, learn before your child leaves for college.

<u>Respect their boundaries</u>: Remember when you were their age? Know that they may not tell you everything or make the same decisions (good or bad) that you did. College life will be significantly different than life as they knew it before. Let them navigate their own way. Be interested and supportive, but don't pry.

<u>Make a life of your own</u>: It is very stressful for college students if they think you will fall apart when they go off to school. Let them know you will miss them, but that your life will be full with work and/or activities.

DeCluttering for the Golden Years

Today, in addition to raising their children, many people are responsible for helping to care for an elderly parent. There are many reasons for seniors to consider getting organized:

- Lifestyle changes (schedules, budgets, social activities)
- Lifetime of accumulation of belongings
- Reclaiming living space
- Inability to care for belongings; too much stuff
- Moving to smaller home; downsizing

Organizing for Safety

Another great benefit of decluttering is that it will ensure your home is safe to navigate.

Keep walkways clear to prevent unnecessary falls. Avoid letting books, magazines or catalogs pile up on the floor;

There are many benefits of getting organized, especially for seniors:

- *Safety*
- *Living more simply and comfortably*
- *Ability to easily get at all the things you need or use*
- *Cash generated/tax deduction by selling or donating unwanted or unused items*

instead, store them on shelves or in baskets--or better yet, pass them on to someone else who might enjoy a good read!

Downsizing to a Smaller Home

Here are some steps you can take to help your family or friends downsize:

*Come along with me as I speak to seniors at Preswick Glen about DeCluttering for the Golden Years. You won't want to miss my valuable advice! Check out organizationmotivation.com, **EPISODE 15, "Spare Room Madness," SEGMENT 2.***

1. Break down the process of downsizing into small pieces -- one drawer, one section of a room at a time.
2. Finish one area or room before you move onto the next.
3. Sort items to keep or donate.
4. Pack to move only those things you definitely have room for in the new home.

But how do you decide what stays and what goes? Here are two questions to ask:
*   Do I absolutely love it?
*   Do I absolutely need it?
If the answer to either of these questions is NO, then it's time to let the item go!

Decluttering your home may take some time, but remember, for every minute spent organizing, an hour is earned. So get started today--you can do it!

CHAPTER 4

DeClutter Your Home

Your home is your sanctuary -- a place where you can escape from the outside world. When you come home, you should feel calm, relaxed, and peaceful. Now, I'm not saying your home has to be perfect, spotless and completely dust-free -- not by a long shot! At our house, we put our feet up on the coffee tables and are used to living with "a little dust." You shouldn't strive for perfection, because nobody can maintain that!

The point of having a home isn't to keep it perfect, it's to be comfortable. You need to feel good when you're in it. I can show you how you can set up systems that work for you and your family to help you have a comfortable, stress-free atmosphere where at the end of the day, you'll be able to relax and put your feet up, too! There should be a place for everything, and everything in its place!

Before we dive in, let's evaluate your situation with a little quiz.

Is CLUTTER Taking Over Your Home?
Take our quiz to find out!

Answer Yes (Y), Sometimes (S) or No (N)

1. How do you feel when you come into your house?
   Are you overwhelmed by clutter?   Y   S   N
   If yes, list the major items that are cluttering your home:

   _____

   _____

   _____

2. Do you have items in your home that are not yours or
   that you inherited? If yes, list these items.   Y   S   N

   _____

   _____

   _____

3. Can you easily find your car keys, cell phone and purse
   every morning?   Y   S   N

4. Do you frequently buy items that you don't really need
   because you love to shop?   Y   S   N

5. Is it difficult for you to let go of sentimental possessions?
                                                         Y   S   N

6. Take a look at your attic, garage or basement. Are they a
   dumping ground for things you don't use or need
   or contain items from your past?   Y   S   N

7. Do you hold on to items that you no longer use because
   you may need to use them later?   Y   S   N

8. Do you have any of your possessions stored at your parents' or other family member's homes?　Y　S　N

9. Are your children mimicking any of your habits- disorganization, over buying, etc?　Y　S　N

10. Do you still have boxes from a prior home that you have never opened?　Y　S　N

11. Do you have any bank or credit card statements that are not needed for tax purposes that are more than three years old?　Y　S　N

12. What's your bedroom like? Is it overcrowded or depressing?　Y　S　N

13. Do you want to get rid of all the items overcrowding your home but are afraid to do so?　Y　S　N

14. Do you have many cleaning and/or beauty products in your bathroom?　Y　S　N

15. Do you buy the latest exercise equipment but lose interest and leave it to take up valuable space in your home?　Y　S　N

16. Do you have a set routine for keeping your house in order?　Y　S　N

17. Is it difficult to see your kitchen counters and table because there is so much kitchen equipment or clutter on top of them?　Y　S　N

18. Do you let your laundry bin overflow before you do the wash?　Y　S　N

19. Do you have a lot of books in your home that you have already read and most likely will not read again?　Y　S　N

20. Have you kept almost every photograph you have taken?　Y　S　N

Score your answers:

Y # _____ x 2 = _____

S # _____ x 1 = _____

N # _____ x 0 = _____

26- 40
Clutter is overwhelming you! It's difficult to function, your mood and energy level is greatly affected. Take a hard, close look at the clutter in your home and take steps to begin to declutter NOW!

11- 25
The clutter in your life is starting to creep up on you. Begin decluttering before it gets overwhelming. Take action now, or it will only get worse and start to affect other areas of your life. Focus on the area that is causing you the most stress first.

10 and under
Congratulations! Clutter is not a major issue. Be careful because it can happen very easily. Get on top of the minor issues now before they get larger. Be proactive!

As we discussed in the first chapter, there are many reasons why people hold on to clutter. And there are just as many positive results when you begin to let go of them. Listen to the difference decluttering the home made to one of my clients who was overwhelmed with extra "stuff".

"I have always been one of those people that saved everything. After years of saving things, my house began overflowing with stuff that would never be used or couldn't be found even if it was needed. After working with Deb to declutter, our house went from a cluttered mess to an organized home that we can enjoy. There have been areas in my home that were so overwhelming, I didn't know where to begin. Therefore, I wouldn't even start. Deb showed me how to change old habits and form new ones. I never thought my house could be presentable. That changed, the day I called Deb! "

Jackie N., homeowner

Can you relate to Jackie's situation? Then read on!

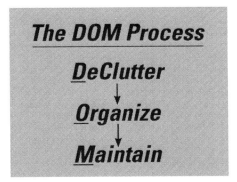

The DOM Process

_D_eClutter
↓
_O_rganize
↓
_M_aintain

You can simplify your life with Deb's DOM process!

The Kitchen

Life is so busy that sometimes we forget to take the time to smell the roses... or a home cooked meal! We all know the benefits of healthy eating, but sometimes our everyday demands make accomplishing it too overwhelming. Combine a busy schedule with a cluttered kitchen and you've got a recipe for disaster!

Getting started is the hardest part!

Reducing clutter in the kitchen will not only lead to calmer meal-times, but healthier eating habits for you and your entire family!

Look around your kitchen and ask yourself these questions:

- Are your cupboards and pantry chock full of food you never use?
- Are unknown foods lurking in your refrigerator or freezer?
- Do you eat or order out more often than you'd like?
- Do you want to cook healthy meals for your family but don't know where to start?

If you answered yes to any (or all!) of these questions, you're not alone. Now is the time to make the commitment to tackle your kitchen. Make it a family project. It's not difficult to create an environment that will motivate you to prepare and serve healthy meals. Getting started is the hardest part!

You won't want to miss my valuable tips and tricks for kitchen decluttering. Watch as I come to the aid of my client Bill, a local business owner, all natural farmer and father of two teenage boys who's in need of a organizing overhaul! Check out organizationmotivation.com, EPISODE 13, "Kitchen Disaster!"

Below are some simple steps to follow to create a kitchen that's fit for healthy cooking and eating.

DeClutter Your Pantry

Step 1 - Empty all the contents of the pantry and place them on the table or countertops sorting like things together (for example: canned good, cereal, pasta).

Step 2 - Toss all food with expired dates. For items that have not expired and you know you will not use, consider donating them to a family member, friend, neighbor or local food pantry.

An organized pantry.

Step 3 - Relocate all non-food items that were in the pantry elsewhere if additional storage areas in the kitchen are available. If not, move them to another area of your home.

Step 4 - Remove all food items from other areas of the kitchen and incorporate them with the sorted food that is on the table or countertops.

Step 5 - Wipe down all shelves so you start with a clean slate.

Step 6 - Put everything back into the pantry arranging like things together with labels facing out. Use baskets, shelf risers and graduated shelves to help create and maintain organization.

DeClutter Your Refrigerator and Freezer

Here's one client's amazing transformation -- her husband thought she bought a new refrigerator without telling him!

Before   *After*

Start by decluttering the front of your refrigerator. Remove all the magnets and notes. Consider installing a bulletin board in another area of the kitchen for these items (see Family Hub, Chapter 1). Even the most organized kitchen looks cluttered if the front of the refrigerator is overcrowded. Repeat the pantry declutter steps for both the refrigerator and freezer.

DeClutter Your Countertops

Create clear and orderly countertops. Only items that are used daily should be out on the counter. Having ample space to prep and cook will motivate you to create healthy meals for your family. To encourage healthy snacking, place fresh fruit in a basket on the countertop.

Before   *After*

Create a Meal Plan

Proper meal planning is critical to healthy eating. Use your meal planning binder (discussed in Chapter 3) to create a meal plan for your family and select ingredients needed for each meal on your computerized grocery list. I recommend that families create a meal plan every two weeks if possible.

Stock Your Kitchen with Healthy Food

Now that your kitchen is primed for success and your meals are planned, stock up on healthy items to make it easy to execute the plan. Purchase fresh in-season fruits and vegetables. Buy healthy staples like rice, beans and broths in bulk when they are on sale.

DeClutter Your Kitchen Table

One declutteing session and this family went from being overwhelmed with paper to enjoying meals together in a peaceful space!

Eating meals together at the table as a family is an important ritual. Declare your kitchen table a no-clutter zone by keeping all unnecessary items off the tabletop.

Being organized in the kitchen is the key to healthy cooking and eating. Take some time today to declutter your kitchen. The time invested will yield significant results and benefits. You'll be glad you did!

Before

After

Bedrooms

Your bedroom should be your sanctuary, a place that is just for you or for you and your partner. If you have clutter in the bedroom, your ability

> **Your bedroom is your sanctuary.**

to relax and to sleep will undoubtedly be affected. Here are some of my rules for keeping the bedroom clutter-free:

Photos: I always tell families that the bedroom is not a place for photos of your children. Now don't get me wrong, I love family photos and have them throughout my entire house -- just not in the bedroom. Restrict photographs to pictures of you and your partner, or scenic shots that make you feel peaceful.

For a really amazing "teen" bedroom transformation, check out the premier episode of Organization Motivation!, at organizationmotivation.com, where we declutter and organize Nick's bedroom, EPISODE 1, SEGMENT 2

<u>Laundry</u>: You may think the overflowing basket of laundry in the corner is not much of a bother, but get rid of it and see how much better you'll feel! Try to stay on top of laundry, or relegate the laundry basket to the bathroom or another area of the house if yours tends to overflow.

<u>Exercise equipment</u>: If at all possible, keep exercise equipment in a different room. The bedroom is not the place for an exercise bike! Usually it ends up becoming another "closet" for your clothes or a place for things to pile up.

<u>Work</u>: Ideally, it would be great to have a separate room in the house for your office, but sometimes that's just not possible. Before we converted one of our rooms into an office for me, the bedroom was the only place for me to store my laptop and work materials. If you must work in the bedroom, relegate all of your items to a specific area and keep it tidy. Better yet, use an armoire or cabinet so that you can shut the doors when you're finished.

<u>Me Time/Couple Time</u>: Make the bedroom a special place for yourself, or for you and your partner. If you're single, think about what makes you happy and what you do to relax. If you like to do your nails, then set up a nail station. If you're married or have a partner, then think about what inspires you to be closer as a couple. Whether it's the ambience details like music or candles or simply something beautiful to look at like a painting or a photograph, choose the items in your bedroom carefully and remember, it's your sanctuary!

"Wish I had contacted The DeClutter Coach sooner! Deb's initial consultation was thorough and allowed me to give her a sense of how we live and what we needed, and she provided some great tips and suggestions. The clutter in the house had become overwhelming and Deb did a great job of helping to prioritize where initial efforts should be focused. Deb and Mary Carole were able to accomplish in two brief sessions what would have taken me far too long to accomplish on my own. The bedroom is now an organized retreat. I'm so glad they were able to help me get a jump start on organizing the rest of the house." **RG, homeowner**

Closets

In my business, I focus on closets a lot. And what I've found is that most people -- women especially -- actually wear only 20 percent of what is in their closet! "I have a ton of clothes, but nothing to wear!" is something I've heard many times!

Your closet should only contain items that you love and that you

actually wear. I had one client who owned 57 pairs of jeans; nobody needs that many! There's no reason to have excess. Instead, you need to focus on what works for you, what you're comfortable in, and what you love.

> **Your closet should only contain clothes that fit and flatter your figure.**

Organizing your closet can have a huge impact on your daily routines. Not only will it make it easier to find clothes that fit and that you enjoy wearing, you'll get a special boost from donating all of the items you no longer use to others who can actually use them. Here's what one of my clients had to say:

"Somehow I feel lighter and more at ease. Can it be that a disorganized closet can also disorient your life? I love my new closet and promise to try and keep it in order. I learned much from you about letting go and that it's only 'stuff.' Once you start sorting, it becomes easy to get rid of unnecessary items.

Want to see how I utilized every inch of space in Cindy's oddly-shaped closet? For more on Cindy's closet declutter and to see the amazing transformation yourself, check out our show at organizationmotivation.com EPISODE 14, "Nothing to Wear?"

The experience truly humbled me into looking at all the clothes and shoes that I never wear but save for someday. My new motto is: Get rid of it! I hope I learned enough to DeClutter on my own, but I know that you are only a phone call away if I need you."

Cindy D.
homeowner and residential client

You can start enjoying all the benefits that Cindy has, too! Here's how:

<u>Step 1</u> - Start by removing everything from the closet. Anything that is not apparel or an accessory - find a new place for it.

<u>Step 2</u> - Sort the clothes in three piles - Keep, Donate/Consign and Toss. Keep - Items that fit and flatter your current figure and that you absolutely love.

Donate/Consign - Items that do not fit or flatter, you do not like and are in good shape. Also, items you have not worn in one year. Put the items right in your car so you remember to bring them to be donated or consigned. If donating, remember to get a receipt so you can claim the deduction on your tax return.

Toss - Items that are stained or torn.

<u>Step 3</u> - When the closet is empty, assess your needs for more efficient closet organization (more rod space, more shelving, a new system). Remember to use all of the closet space - floor to ceiling.

<u>Step 4</u> - In a neat and orderly fashion, return your keep items into the closet, starting with the hanging items. Consider using matching hangers. Wooden and huggable hangers work well at preserving the shape of your clothes and create a uniform appearance in your closet. Organize hanging clothes by type (shirt: long-sleeved, short-sleeved, tanks, camisole, pants: jeans, dress pants, then dresses, skirts and jackets/blazers) Within each category, arrange by color - light to dark. This will speed up outfit coordination in the morning.

<u>Step 5</u> - For folded items, use baskets, bins or shelf dividers for better organization. Label for ease of recognition. Bulky sweaters take up less room when folded.

Step 6 - For shoes, use clear plastic labeled shoe bins. The bins are inexpensive, protect your shoes so they will last longer and help maintain a visually organized closet. What's the sense of buying an expensive pair of shoes if you're going to throw them on the floor to get dusty? Invest in shoe bins, and take care of the shoes you own!

Step 7 - For accessories (scarves, belts, jewelry) use hanging organizing or stackable products. There are so many affordable organizing products on the market. Easy access is key.

Step 8 - A mirror is a must have in or near your closet. Also have in close proximity the following items: a pair of scissors, safety pins, a lint brush and a shoe buffing sponge.

Things to Remember to Maintain an Organized Closet

1. Every time you wear an item, after it is washed or dry cleaned, return the item on the hanger in the closet, hanging it on the rod in the opposite direction. This will force you to utilize more of your clothes. In six months to one year, if all of the hangers are not turned in the opposite direction, it means you haven't worn the item and probably won't wear it – so it needs to go!

2. Before shopping, take stock of what you already own. Also, get to know what styles look good on you and work well with your figure and stick with them.

3. For every new item you purchase, remove one item from the closet. With some clients, the ratio of "one in, one out" should be closer to "one in, five out!" Some people may not be happy with that direction, but after all, I'm there to help them declutter their lives!

4. After you wear, wash or dry clean it - put it away! Avoid putting clothes on the floor, the chair or the treadmill.

With just a little bit of time and effort, you'll see an amazing difference. So what are you waiting for? Give it a try today!

Bathrooms

I love to help people organize their medicine cabinets, because they are notorious for collecting clutter. Take some time to sort through yours, and only keep the items that you use often. If you take multiple medications each day, purchase a pill container to help you keep them in order. Remember to check expiration dates on all your medicines, and promptly discard any that have expired. Important tip: do not flush unused medicines down the toilet, as they can contaminate groundwater. Instead, mix them with an unpalatable substance, such as kitty litter or coffee grounds, seal in a bag, and throw in the trash.

Go green! Use towels two days before washing them. We use an over-the-door rack to hang towels and then put them into the laundry basket after the second day.

Here's another quick tip: keep a permanent marker in the bathroom to help you track expiration dates. Mark the month and year on your makeup, circle expiration dates on medicines, etc. It's easy to forget these things and wind up with many expired products cluttering up your bathroom spaces.

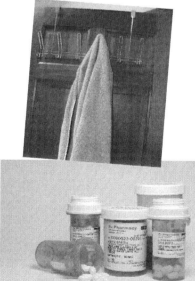

Laundry

Set up an efficient place to do laundry. Some people have the luxury of a laundry room; however, a workable laundry area can be created in a very small space. You need a neat

> **What you own, owns you!**

place to store all of your laundry products, such as detergent, bleach, stain remover, fabric softener, etc. You also need a place to fold clothes and story dirties that are waiting to be washed.

Here's a great laundry tip: towels seem to multiply in the wash. We recommend giving each family member his or her own color towel. They are responsible for folding and putting away the towels that are theirs!

Playrooms

Keeping an organized playroom or play area is a great way to help your children learn the benefits of organization and responsibility.

The first thing to remember is to tailor the room to the age of the children. Keep only toys that they currently play with and use. As I tell my clients, "what you own, owns you!" Do your children really need dozens of toy trucks? If your child has five that he or she will play with and treasure, isn't that better than 50 that will get neglected and thrown around? Rotate the toys that are out for play every week

Before   *After*

or two so that there's always something new and interesting. Store items that they're not ready for in a different area, and donate anything they've outgrown.

If you save everything, then nothing has value.

There are all sorts of storage units, bins and toy boxes for storing toys. However, you don't have to go out and buy the most expensive items to have an organized area. It's just about making it work for you and your kids. We work with clients and help them utilize things they already have in their home to help get them organized.

Involve your children in putting away toys -- even at a very young age, they'll be eager to help! Here's a fun tip to help them sort: take a photograph of the toys you're storing and laminate it or tape it to the toy bin. When it's time to clean up, your child will be able to easily locate where the item goes. As your children grow, you can add the word beneath the picture. This is great for storing all kinds of toys -- blocks, dolls, cars, anything with smaller pieces!

Involving your children with organization from an early age encourages their analytical skills and teaches them the value of responsibility and the pride of accomplishments.

"You have no idea how nice the mood of the house has been since Syd, our 10-year-old, began to feel better about her space. She is definitely affected by the new calm she now feels as a result of her declutter experience! Thank you so much! We are very much looking forward to your next visit."

Chris C., homeowner

To see more on Syd's amazing transformation, check out "Organization Motivation!" at organizationmotivation.com "Cute Disaster," EPISODE 2 SEGMENT 4

Artwork and Other Paper

When it comes to childrens' artwork and other papers, I always remind my clients, "If you save everything, then nothing has value." It simply is not necessary to save every single test, book report, or picture your child has ever brought

home from school. All these papers will do is pile up and create more clutter, and you'll never look back at them later!

Instead, choose a few special papers or documents to hold onto and file them for safekeeping. Years later, you'll enjoy looking back at them. Another good tip is to take a photo of your child with some of his or her artwork, awards, certificates, etc. and then let the paper copy go.

Giving Back

Whether you're sifting through papers or deciding which toys to donate, it's important to involve your children in the process. Teach them from an early age to give back and let them help when you declutter, and they'll learn the importance of compassion and giving to others.

Here's a great tip for birthday parties: in lieu of presents, ask friends to bring a toy to donate, or to make a contribution to a local nonprofit organization. You'll save yourself clutter, and everyone will feel great about helping an important cause!

When my children were young, I always talked to them about the importance of letting some of their toys go so that other children who were not as fortunate could enjoy them. Before birthdays and holidays, we would routinely go through our toys to make room for the new ones and donate the rest. Not only did it help us keep the toys under control, we all felt good about giving to others. When you teach your kids these lessons from a young age, the importance of giving back will stay with them their entire lives.

Garage

Garages can very easily turn into dumping grounds. One of my clients, Mary, used her garage in place of attic and basement storage.

The result? A two-stall garage that she hadn't parked in for more than ten years! My team and I spent a day helping her declutter, and after removing more than 2,000 pounds of unnecessary "stuff" and reorganizing the things she kept, we were all able to cheer her on as she parked her car in its stall! Here's what Mary had to say about her garage declutter:

Before

After

"It was an amazing experience, and it was not as difficult emotionally as I thought it would be. You know, when you accumulate things, there's a sentimental value that goes along with them. But for some of these things, knowing that they've been here, and I haven't used them, and apparently I really didn't need them, it was so easy to just let go!"

Regardless of what you store in your garage, it's important to have a method of organization that will make it easy to find the things you need -- and get them back into place when you're done! Here are some of my favorite tips for keeping an orderly garage.

To see more on Mary's garage, check out organizationmotivation.com, EPISODE 18, "Garage Transformation!"

Tip # 1 - Declutter first!

If your children gave up hockey years ago, why keep around that large net, four hockey sticks and the huge equipment bag that still contains their smelly old pads (I have personal experience with this unfortunately). The bottom line is, if an item in your garage has not been used in a year or is broken and not able to be

Everything has a place, and everything in its place!

repaired- it's clutter and it has to go! If the item is in good shape, consider donating or consignment. Remove it now from your space to make room for the things your family needs and uses on a regular basis.

Tip #2 - Decide on an organization method.

Some ideas are: sorting by family member, activity or type. For example, you can have a shelf or bin for each child, each activity or each type of item. There are a wide variety of organizational products available for garages, and many sporting goods stores or online sites offer products specifically for sporting goods. Check out all of the options before you make a decision. It's amazing the excellent options they have for bikes, golf bags and even skis. Do your research before you buy!

Tip #3 - Use clear plastic containers for storage.

Some people, like my client Mary, need the garage for storage space. It's important to protect your items from moisture and mold. If you're storing items in your garage that are susceptible to the elements, clear plastic containers will keep them airtight and safe while allowing you to see what's inside. Be sure to label all bins for quick and easy retrieval.

Tip #4 - Create a plan for where everything will go.

A place for everything and everything in its place makes it easy to maintain the system. Use labels, hooks, bins, etc. to encourage putting items back where they belong after they are used.

Tip # 5 - Keep like things together.

Once you have decided on your organization method and created a plan, it's important to keep like things together. For example, keep all your tools, gardening materials, car repair items, sporting goods, etc. in the same spots so that they are easy to locate when you need them!

"I just wanted to let you know how much I appreciate the advice you gave us at the Dunham Public Library talk. I have been struggling with the excess for a long, long time and was able to really make some headway last week. I used your rule about taking everything out first, especially in the garage and the spare room. That worked great! Thank you for giving me the boost I needed to

start going in the right direction. I look forward to learning more and continuing to make positive efforts to declutter."

Linda M., homeowner

Moving

Moving to a new home? There's no better time to declutter! From selling your home faster to ensuring a quick and easy transition to your new place, we've got you covered. Read on to find out how to create an organization plan for your move that will save you money and time! (Relocating your office? See Chapter 6 for more on corporate moves!)

> *If you fail to plan, you plan to fail!*

DeCluttering your Home for a Faster Sale

If you plan to sell your home, it must present better than the competition. People need to imagine living there -- and that means it's time to declutter! When a home is filled with clutter, people see the clutter and not the home. It also says two things: the rooms are too small and there is not enough storage.

However, when a home is clutter free, rooms look larger and are more appealing. It appears that there is enough storage and living space for a family.

Some general tips to keep in mind:
- Remove excess clutter from all rooms, closets, basement, garage and attic.
- Remove all personal photos and knick knacks.
- Remove excess furniture.

Kitchens and baths sell a home. Concentrate on those areas when decluttering; remove clutter from countertops, pantries and closets.

Decluttering your home has another benefit -- it will make your moving process much easier! Why take items that you no longer use or need with you?

Planning Your Move
1. Label each box with the contents and the room it belongs.
2. Write a manifest: list all of your boxes and include info on what they contain
3. Instruct movers to place boxes in the appropriate rooms at the new home. That way you won't end up with a huge pile that you have to sort yourself!

From bedrooms to closets to garages, remember: you must have a plan to be successful.

You can do it!

CHAPTER 5

DeClutter Your Finances

John was a small business owner who called me after he heard one of my radio interviews. Frustrated with the clutter in his office and his struggling finances, he was at the end of his rope. The first step was to tackle the unbelievable mounds of stuff all over his desk. Once we cleared up the paperwork and set up a filing system, it was time to get to the root of the problem: John had "financial clutter." After I examined his finances, it quickly became apparent that he lacked any sort of organizational system to keep track of his bills and expenses. There was no way for him to tell where his money was going! Once I helped him establish some efficient ways to keep track of his invoices, billing dates, and the money coming in and going out, his business skyrocketed!

Time and again, I have found that there is a direct correlation between people who have clutter and people who have mismanaged finances. It's time to cut the "financial clutter" and start taking steps to improve your finances! Let's start with some questions:

Financial Health Self-Assessment Questions

- Have you established a budget and do you follow it?
- Do you know exactly how much debt you have?
- Is a significant amount of your debt credit card debt?
- Do you consistently spend more money than you make?
- Do you pay bills late more often than you pay them on time?
- Do you balance your checkbook each month?
- Do you have a savings account that you add to on a regular basis?
- Do you have any retirement savings?
- Are you savings for your children's college education?
- Do you sometimes wonder where all your money goes?
- Do you plan before you spend?
- Do you use coupons?

Set up and Stay on a Budget

Where is your money going? A powerful exercise is to record every penny you spend for an entire month. This includes any checks you write, credit cards you use or cash you spend. Some people are very surprised when they see the results of this exercise. It's important to know where you are today so you can move toward a better tomorrow!

It takes about 30 minutes to an hour to set up a budget. Here's How:

1. Collect all financial documents including bank statements, pay stubs and bills/statements.

2. List monthly net income from all sources- full and/or part time job(s), child support, interest, etc.

3. List all monthly expenses- this should include everything you spend money on including: rent/mortgage, groceries, utilities (gas/ electric, phone, water, trash pick-up), cable, spending money/allowance, clothing, credit card payments,

insurance, car payments and expenses including gas and repair costs, gifts, medical/dental expenses, entertainment, savings, retirement plan, college savings etc.

4. Divide the expenses into two categories: fixed and variable. Fixed expenses are those that stay about the same every month (rent/mortgage, car payment) Variable expenses are those that can change on a monthly basis (groceries, clothing) This category will be important when adjustments need to be made.

5. Total monthly income and expenses. If your expenses are greater than your income, immediate adjustments will need to be made. Most adjustments will need to be made to the variable expenses. If the situation is extreme,  adjustments may need to be made to the fixed expenses such as selling your home or car to purchase a more affordable option or you may have to take on a second job to increase your income.

6. Review your budget often. Keep track of the actual expenses and compare them to the budget. Make adjustments where necessary. Reviewing your budget often will help you stay on track.

Credit Cards

Use your credit cards wisely, and you can eliminate credit card debt! Your goal should be to pay your credit cards off each month to avoid paying interest on your purchases.

If you have credit card debt, do your best to get it paid off as soon as possible. Here are some tips to help you do that:

1. Pay more than the minimum payment every month.
2. Try to consolidate all debt to one lower rate interest card. If you cannot do that, pay off the balance on the highest interest rate card first.
3. Try to re-negotiate the terms of your agreements with your creditors. Some may be willing to reduce your interest rates.
4. Seek advice from an Accountant, Financial Planner or a non-profit debt service such as Consumer Credit Counseling Service.

How's Your Credit Rating?

Get your FREE credit report annually. Each of the three credit bureaus (Equifax, Experian & Transunion) are required to provide you with one free credit report annually. Visit annualcreditreport.com.

Know Your FICO Score

Your FICO Score is a credit scoring model that represents your creditworthiness. A score of 720 and up should be your goal. Transunion offers a free seven day trial from one of their subsidiaries – Zen Dough which will give you your FICO score for free.

Saving for the Future

Whether for your children's college education or your retirement, saving a small amount of money every week can add up over time. If you don't save now, then start small, but start now!

Here's some tips to help you start saving:

1 – Spend less than you make

Start small, but start NOW!

2 – Pay yourself first- direct deposit a certain amount of money every paycheck to your 401K, savings or investment account or 529 College Savings Plan. You won't miss what you don't have!
3 – Eat out less
4 – Use coupons
5 – Buy only when you absolutely need something
6 – Buy used and save the difference

Here is a website that offers a calculator to help you plan if you are saving for a specific goal. www.lifetuner.org/topics/25-saving/tools/save-foragoal#

Spend Wisely and Save Money: Customer Loyalty Cards

My job often requires me to travel out of state, and my family and I are big on taking vacations, too. Staying in hotels across the country is fun, but it can get expensive -- unless you know how to make your money work for you! I can honestly say that I rarely pay out-of-pocket for my hotel expenses, thanks to my customer loyalty credit card. I earn points for everything I spend, which translate into free stays at my favorite hotels.

Customer loyalty cards aren't just for hotels, however. These days, credit cards are available with rewards ranging from cash back to gift cards or other rewards. An Internet search can bring up dozens of different types of rewards cards. Do some research and find the one that works for you. Make your money work for you, and earn something back in the meantime!

For more of my advice on decluttering your finances, catch my show, "Organization Motivation!" at organizationmotivation.com. You won't want to miss EPISODE 10, "Organize Your Finances and Legal Documents," and EPISODE 19, "Financial DeClutter," Segment 1.

CHAPTER 6

Streamline and Simplify at Work

Here's a question: would you walk into work with a splotch of mustard on your dress? How about pasta sauce spilled down your shirt and tie? Of course you wouldn't! The way you dress and present yourself is all part of your image, and when you're in a professional environment you take careful measures to look and act a certain way.

So if you would never think of wearing slippers to work, then how could you consider it acceptable to have a cluttered, messy, or disorganized office? Like your clothes, your desk and workspace is a reflection of you -- and it's important to always present yourself in the best possible light!

How DeCluttering and Organizing Affects Work

Here's something else to think about: the way you organize your office isn't just about appearances. It goes much deeper than that. Are you as productive and efficient as you can be at work? Can a disorganized business really have a negative impact on your bottom line? You bet it can. Disorganization robs you of your time, your effectiveness and your credibility. If you end each day feeling stressed, tired, or anxious, don't worry -- you're not alone!

In my corporate business, DC Efficiency Consulting, we routinely work with busy organizations and their employees to improve workflow systems, provide training, and motivate workers to be more productive at their jobs. The training sessions, workshops, employee wellness programs, keynote addresses, and other corporate services that we provide help businesses and their employees identify the areas they need to work on, streamline, and simplify processes in order to do their jobs more efficiently. Many employees take the information they learn in the work place about getting organized and managing their time better and apply it to their home and family life.

Here's what some of my clients have had to say after taking some time to focus on these important topics:

"Before Coach Deb, my office looked and felt like it was ready to pop, it was so full of stacks of papers and project files and junk! She came in like a whirlwind, helped me get everything squared away, and now my colleagues and visitors really notice the difference. It has made our operations even more efficient, and it has had the side effect of creating a nicer space for our team to do creative work together. Thanks Deb!"

Matthew S.
Director of Marketing & Communications
at Mohawk Valley Community College

"While the Boilermaker boasts a volunteer staff of thousands, our staff is very small. Managing all those people is a challenge that demands efficiency. Being in our building for over eleven years we saw an accumulation of 'stuff' cluttering up what little storage space we had. Deb came in and decluttered and organized our office area clearly making us a more efficient organization. Her let's roll up our sleeves and do this attitude is infectious. Races are all about time. Thank you Deb for giving some of ours back! "

Timothy R.
Executive Director, Boilermaker Road Race
& National Distance Running Hall of Fame

"After Deb's enthusiastic and informative presentation on Time Management, our Staffworks Corporate Office Team was definitely ready to DECLUTTER! Since I was one of the greatest contributors to our office clutter, I led by example, rolled up my sleeves and dug right in. We worked for at least two weeks purging, boxing and storing files while also tackling closets and stor-

age areas. This physical exercise refreshed our goal to minimize the handling of paper documents by "going electronic" whenever possible. What a refreshing change it was for us to PURGE rather than accumulate. The results of Deb's presentation are visible in the overall office-scape and in individual office spaces. Some of the team carried her sage advice a step further and applied their refreshed attitudes toward organizing into their homes. Building efficiencies and effectively using our time at work and home will always be an on-going effort. THANK YOU to Deb for raising our awareness regarding the importance such results have on business productivity and personal peace. In a world of challenging schedules and budgets, Deb's program was definitely a worthwhile investment of our time and resources."

Anita V.
President, Staffworks Corporate Office

"The Declutter Coach is fabulous. Deb came to my house to help me overhaul my home office. It was September. The space had been a dumping ground all summer. In a short time of a couple hours the office was in perfect order. I am still able to maintain the space thanks to Deb's suggestions. I highly recommend the Declutter Coach!"

Tracy R.
New Hartford, NY

Watch me as I help one accomplished artist declutter his home office! Check out "Organization Motivation!" at organizationmovitivation.com, EPISODE 6, "Artistically Organized Holiday," SEGMENT 1! You'll be amazed!

Productivity and Efficiency Quiz

Before we get started on how you can increase productivity and decrease stress levels, it's time for some self-reflection on why you're not achieving all your work-related goals. Take our quiz to find out more.

Answer "yes" or "no" to the questions on the following page.

Clutter

1. My workspace is messy and disorganized. It makes me feel stressed and overwhelmed.   Y   N
2. I usually cannot find my keys and/or cell phone and often lose important documents and phone numbers.   Y   N
3. I need more storage space.   Y   N

Paper

1. I do not file paper because I won't be able to find it when I need it.   Y   N
2. Most of the time, my desk is stacked with paper and files. Y   N
3. I am afraid to throw anything away and have a hard time managing paper.   Y   N

Time

1. Often, I miss important deadlines.   Y   N
2. Sometimes I am late for appointments or meetings and arrive unprepared.   Y   N
3. Because I can't remember where I put items, I waste time looking for things.   Y   N

Procrastination

1. Usually I procrastinate and work on tasks or projects right before they are due.   Y   N
2. I delay working on tasks that I don't like to do.   Y   N
3. Several times a day I check email rather than tackle a large or difficult project.   Y   N

Quiz Scoring

1 - 3 Yes answers
Great job. You are working efficiently and feeling in control.

4 - 6 Yes answers
There are a few areas that need tweaking. Handle one at a time. Set up a few new systems and routines and monitor your progress.

7 - 8 Yes answers
You have to be feeling frustrated, overwhelmed and stressed out. But

don't give up! Tackle the most stressful area first. Take action as soon as possible so you can get on the right track.

9 or More Yes answers
Your work life is in chaos. Take action immediately! Begin digging out and setting up new systems today. Consistency is key to take back control. Ask a trusted friend or family member to be your Accountability Buddy.

Most employees waste one hour per day due to a disorganized workspace or inefficient time management skills.

Getting Started

You can be more productive and efficient at work! Many people feel overwhelmed and don't know where to start, so it's important to take things one step at a time. As I always tell my clients, small changes over time yield big results!

We're going to discuss some main points to help you get organized, increase productivity, and manage your time better.

This business owner's desk went from disorganized and overwhelming to orderly and inspiring.

Declutter Your Workspace

A cluttered space creates a cluttered mind. Clear your workspace and your focus and creativity will soar!

Whether you work at a small desk, a cubicle or a spacious office, the same rules apply for keeping your workspace organized. Decluttering

Want to see me helping more employees decluttering their offices? Check out "Organization Motivation!" EPISODE 9, "Corporate Launch," SEGMENTS 1 & 2 and EPISODE 12, "Director's Dilemma," SEGMENTS 1 & 2. You won't believe your eyes!

and getting organized will help you be more productive, feel more in control and less stressed. You will be able to retrieve items you need quickly and your work-space will go from disorganized and overwhelming to orderly and inspiring!

Steps for DeCluttering Your Workspace

<u>The DOM Process - DeClutter, Organize, Maintain</u>

DeClutter

Start with your desktop. Desktops are for working, not piling! Then do the same for your desk drawers, credenza or other areas of your workspace.

Digging Out from the Paper Clutter

<u>Evaluate the piles</u>

Typically most desktop clutter is about 1/3 items that need action and 2/3 things that need to be filed or thrown away. As you go through each item, quickly sort them into two categories- action items or things to file. Anything that needs to be thrown away- do it immediately. Have a wastebasket near by and remember anything with personal or business sensitive information needs to be shredded.

Not sure what to toss? Here are a few questions to ask yourself: Will it help me meet my job responsibilities and goals? If there a legal reason why I need to keep it? Is the information current? Can I access the information on-line?

Now carefully review the action pile and add the tasks to a To Do List estimating how long each task will take. Then, add up all the hours of work you have.

<u>Pare it down</u>

Try to reduce the items on your To Do list that are not critical. File all the paper on the desk in folders that are easy to access. The To Do list now replaces your action pile. There is no longer a need for the paper to be in view. When you are ready to tackle an item on your To Do list, take out the necessary file and begin working.

<u>Toss vs. Keep</u>

Shred any documents containing personal or sensitive info. Some questions to ask yourself: Are their tax or legal reasons to keep it? Will it help me meet my goals? Does it tie in with the core responsibilities of my job? Is the information up to date? Could I get it from somewhere or someone else if I needed it?

Step 1: Remove all items from the area

Step 2: While removing the items, sort them by category- desk supplies pens, pencils) and accessories (filing trays, memo holder), filing materials, items to be filed, current projects, knickknacks, etc.

Step 3: Toss anything that you no longer need. Do not organize what you can toss. Not sure what to toss? Ask yourself these questions: Why do I need this? It is current or relevant to my work? How often will I use or need it? Can I get it from someone or somewhere else?

Step 4: Wipe down the entire surface so you are starting with a clean slate.

Organize

Step 1: Decide what will go back in the area. On your desktop, keep only those items that you use everyday and limit the amount. Visual clutter breeds mental clutter! Leave clear space on your desktop for writing purposes and to give your desk a neat appearance. Remember - create a space for everything and keep everything in its place.

Step 2: Keep the items you use most often closest to you. They should be within reach and take precedence in your workspace. For example- keep a pen and memo pad near the phone.

Step 3: Use space saving organizing products for supplies and stacking trays for papers you need to refer to on a daily basis. They are an efficient use of desk space. Keep like things together.

Step 4: Photos and knick-knacks create a personalized space, but keep them to a minimum.

Step 5: Switch to a wireless keyboard and mouse. You'll be surprised at what a difference this can make. Visually your space will feel and look neater.

Step 6: To prevent paper clutter on your desk, it's important to have an efficient filing system. Keep in mind filing systems are for retrieval, not storage. They should be simple and consistent. Create an Action file for things you plan to do within the next day or two. Keep only active files at your workspace. Most people refer to only 20% of the items they save. Think before you file!

Maintain - Tips for Staying Organized

- Begin using a Daily Planner and a To Do List. Record all meetings, tasks, deadlines and notes in your planner.

- Organizing your schedule and tasks in one place will minimize paper and sticky notes- both culprits of desk clutter.

- If a task takes less than two minutes, just do it! If it takes more than two minutes, put it on your To Do List and file the paper in your action file.

- Make a habit of handling a piece of paper only once. Make a decision to act on it, file it or toss it. Don't put it in a pile and hope to get to it later. Procrastination causes clutter!

- Use it, then put it away. Whether it's a file, report, book or stapler. Get in the habit of putting things away when you're done with them. Don't wait until later, because later never comes. It is more efficient to stay organized as you work.

- Clear your desk at the end of every workday. It will ensure a fresh start tomorrow. Having an organized workspace creates energy and motivation. Give it a try!

"I was more than pleased to see the motivation that Deb Cabral sparked in all my staff. Many workers started the next work day clearing out paper clutter. As a team we will work on organizing our time to be more efficient with all the tips that were presented to us. What I had hoped to stimulate for my staff by providing this workshop happened to a greater extent than I imagined. I am looking forward to a more organized work environment and for staff to be more efficient and productive. Thank You Deb!"

Linda M.
Director of Supportive Case Management
at The Neighborhood Center Inc.

Improve Your Time Management

Today's economy is forcing businesses to do more with less in order to stay competitive. Using time wisely is not only a benefit - it's a necessity! Managing time effectively is a skill that can increase productivity and the bottom line.

Julie Morgenstern in her book, *Time Management from the Inside Out*, (2004, St Martin's Press) says that in order to manage your time better, you need to think of it as something tangible, rather than intangible. She suggests that it is easier to manage your time if you think of it as something you can see, just as you would if you were organizing your kitchen pantry or bedroom closet. I agree!

Our team works with many busy clients who feel that there is simply not enough time in the day to accomplish everything. To get started, we have them write down their schedule as well as their To Do list. We actually block it out on paper, hour by hour so they have a visual picture of what their day will look like. Many clients indicate they had been keeping all this information in their head hoping to remember it all or on bits of paper here, there and every where. That's enough to give you a headache!

After many years of working in corporate America, attending numerous classes, reading several books on the subject of time management and working with my clients, I believe there are a few key components to improve how you manage your time. In this chapter you will hear my easy to follow tips for doing just that! Right now I want you to keep a positive attitude and an open mind. You CAN manage your time better. With hard work, determination and consistency you will be on the road to increased productivity and less stress.

Three Key Tips to Help Manage Time Effectively

1 - Create a plan

Everyone has heard the slogan, "Plan your work, then work your plan". However, only a small percentage of people actually do it. The key to success in almost anything, including managing your time better is to have a plan.

Research shows that multitasking can slow you down!

As it relates to work, it is important to know what are doing and how you are going to do it. Equally important is to know how long it is going to take. Unfortunately, this is where most people fall short. They are ineffective at measuring how long a specific task will take and therefore to not plan enough time to complete the task. Lastly, you need to know when the task needs to be completed.

2 - Record it

I'm sure you have heard before that you are more likely be successful at reaching a goal or completing a task if you write it down. It can be on paper or digitally- your choice. The key is the actual recording of the item whether it be writing your To Do list or scheduling a meeting.

3 - Be consistent!

Consistency is critical to success when it comes to time management. If creating a plan and recording it are considered the training and foundation of becoming a good time manager, then being consistent is what closes the deal! It's the most important part of the equation.

Manage Your Time Effectively - Create a Plan

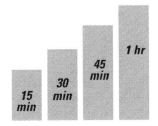

Determine how long a task will take to complete

In order to become effective at managing your time better, you will need to become efficient at figuring out how long a task takes to complete. The only way to do this is to practice.

For the next few weeks, on your daily To Do list indicate the amount of time you believe it will take you to complete each task. After the task is done, in another color pen, indicate the actual time it took to complete the task. Were you on target? Where there certain tasks that took longer than you thought? Were there tasks that you were able to complete sooner than anticipated? If the task is something you do not like to do, did it take you longer?

After a few weeks, you will have a good idea of the amount of time it will take you to complete most of the tasks on your To Do list.

One thing to keep in mind is that the amount of time it takes you to complete a task may be different from someone else. If you manage employees, ask them to do this exercise and share their results with you.

GOALS:
What you want to achieve

TASKS:
The way to achieve a goal, how you get there

Determine Your Job Responsibilities

One of the first things I do when I am working one on one with an individual is to ask them to articulate the major responsibilities of their job. I also ask them to list them in priority order. Believe it or not, many people cannot do that. Can you?

List the major responsibilities of your job in priority order:

1. _____

2. _____

3. _____

4. _____

If you are having trouble with this exercise, review your job description or meet with your manager. It's difficult to manage your time and tasks better if you are not sure what is expected of you.

Determine Your Goals

Once you have determined your major responsibilities in priority order, you need to set specific goal(s) for each responsibility.

Set a specific goal(s) for each responsibility above. *Goals must be clearly defined.*

1. _____

2. _____

3. _____

4. _____

Turn Goals into Tasks and Schedule Them

THEN...
- Divide each goal into specific tasks
- List tasks for each goal; schedule tasks on daily To Do list
- Review goals daily - it will keep you motivated and focused
- Re-assess, re-prioritize and evaluate balance between responsibilities/ goals/tasks

RESPONSIBILITIES
↓
GOALS
↓
TASKS
↓
SCHEDULE

Creating an Effective Filing System

Here are some steps to follow to create an effective filing system. Filing is for retrieval, not storage so think before you file. In order to be able to manage your time better, you need to be able to quickly retrieve items that you've filed.

Follow these tips:
- Decide on a system of categories and labeling
- Use wording that makes sense to you and will be easy to find later
- Color code files (financial, employee, etc.)
- Keep most often used files at your desk
- Alphabetize or arrange in an order that makes sense to you
- File everyday. Do not let paper hang around - clutter breeds clutter!
- Weed files often
- Limit files to two drawers

Paperwork
Schedule time daily to process paperwork - this is a MUST

Maintain
Maintain an organized workspace - a few minutes a day can make the difference.

Plan Ahead
Use the last 15 minutes of each workday to plan tomorrow's work

Review
Review your plan periodically and make adjustments where necessary

Manage Your Time Effectively – Record it

    I once worked with a successful attorney who ended each day feeling overwhelmed, stressed, and frustrated. In order to assess the core of his problems, I asked him to write a to-do list of the tasks he wanted to get accomplished each day. After he wrote it, I asked him to assign a time amount next to each task, estimating how long it would take to complete. When he finished and I added up the times, he was astounded to find that his to-do list was 37 ½ hours long! There's not enough time in the day! Realizing this allowed him to refocus his priorities and create to-do lists with fewer items that he could reasonably accomplish each day. Instead of 30 items on his list that he could never accomplish, he cut the number down to seven or eight that he could manage. The results, he told me, were "life-changing." He now ends his day feeling a sense of accomplishment, not frustration.

Sample to do list:

Your Name

DATE

meetings:

call

meetings and calls to be made for that day

List for tasks and boxes to check off to show progress

Plenty of space to jot notes throughout the day

to do list ©2012, 484 Design, Inc.

As I mentioned earlier, studies show you are more likely to achieve a goal and/or complete a task if you write it down. Here are the basic steps to writing an effective To Do List.

Write an Effective To Do List

1. Categorize your to do's (or tasks) keeping like things together (ex- making phone calls, preparing reports, writing letters or e-mails)
2. Prioritize the items on your to do list so you know what is critical
3. Put a time estimate of how long it will take to complete next to each task
4. Review your to do list periodically during the day and re-assess and re-prioritize when necessary
5. If you have the same to do's on a weekly, daily or monthly basis, consider putting them on your computer so you can update them and print them easily. See sample to do list on the previous page.

Benefits of an Effective To Do List

- Helps meet goals and objectives
- Makes it easy to stay on track or get back on track when you've been interrupted
- Lets you put like tasks together to be more efficient
- Saves times by helping to prioritize tasks
- Reduces stress as you don't have to worry about forgetting an important task
- Gives a sense of accomplishment when you can cross something off

Choosing the Right Planner – Paper vs. Digital

Equally as important as writing an effective To Do List is setting up and maintaining a Daily Planner. This is an important tool in helping you plan and manage your day. I suggest you use one planner for all of your family and work appointments and tasks. It's hard to agree to work late to help your boss finish a project if you can't remember if your child has a baseball game. Many

Paper clutter is often a symptom of poor time management rather than poor organizing skills. The Wall Street Journal reports that most workers waste about an hour a day looking for items on cluttered desk and in poorly organized files.

of our clients had separate planners for home and work and found themselves in this situation or checked the wrong calendar. It's much more efficient to use one and separate family from work by color-coding.

The options for planners are endless! Whether you select paper or digital, the choice is yours. What is most important is ease of use and making the commitment to be consistent. Below is some information to help you make the decision as to which planner is right for you.

<u>Paper</u>

Pros
- Easy to set up
- Doesn't need charging
- Easy to go back and forth between pages

Cons
- Others cannot access your schedule
- Cannot be backed up
- Cannot search

<u>Digital</u>

Pros
- Easy to search by date, name or word
- Others can access your schedule and you can access theirs
- Small and easy to carry

Cons
- Needs to be charged, some run out of charge quickly
- May not be as easy to view as paper

Below is a sample daily planner page:

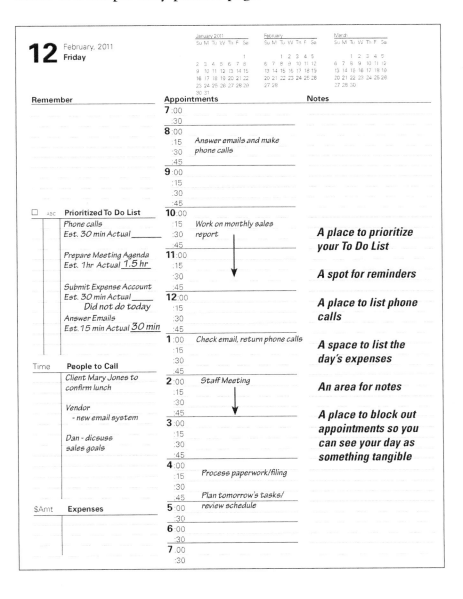

12 February, 2011
Friday

January 2011	February	March
Su M Tu W Th F Sa	Su M Tu W Th F Sa	Su M Tu W Th F Sa

Remember

Appointments   **Notes**

7 :00
:30
8 :00
:15   Answer emails and make
:30   phone calls
:45
9 :00
:15
:30
:45

☐ ABC **Prioritized To Do List**   **10** :00
Phone calls   :15   Work on monthly sales
Est. 30 min Actual _____   :30   report   *A place to prioritize*
     :45   *your To Do List*
Prepare Meeting Agenda   **11** :00
Est. 1hr Actual *1.5 hr*   :15   *A spot for reminders*
     :30
Submit Expense Account   :45
Est. 30 min Actual _____   **12** :00   *A place to list phone*
   Did not do today   :15   *calls*
Answer Emails   :30
Est. 15 min Actual *30 min*   :45
     1 :00   Check email, return phone calls
     :15   *A space to list the*
     :30   *day's expenses*
Time   **People to Call**   :45
Client Mary Jones to   **2** :00   Staff Meeting
confirm lunch   :15   *An area for notes*
     :30
Vendor   :45
  - new email system   **3** :00   *A place to block out*
     :15   *appointments so you*
Dan - dicsuss   :30   *can see your day as*
sales goals   :45   *something tangible*
     4 :00
     :15   Process paperwork/filing
     :30
     :45   Plan tomorrow's tasks/
$Amt   **Expenses**   **5** :00   review schedule
     :30
     6 :00
     :30
     7 :00
     :30

Manage Your Time Effectively - Be Consistent

Consistency is key in helping you come an effective time manager. A great way to be consistent is to develop routines. I've created the LEAF Process to help you do just that!

The LEAF Process to DeClutter Your Worklife and Manage Your Daily Schedule and Tasks

List
all your tasks, meetings, appointments, phone calls, projects all in one reliable place, preferably your Planner. Write down tasks in your planner on the day you plan to do them.

Estimate
How long each task will take. Break down large tasks into smaller tasks that are easier to calculate, then add up how long it will take you. Schedule tasks where there is enough time in your schedule.

Adopt an Action Plan
Decide how and when the tasks will be handled: Immediate, delegate, schedule and do at a late date.

Follow Through
Plan your work, then work your plan. Put your plan into action. Complete the tasks on the day you plan to. Start and finish a project when you say you will.

Determine when and how you do your best work
Everyone works differently. We have different likes and dislikes, styles, habits and energy levels. Some people can work quickly and efficiently without error. Others need to take their time to ensure accuracy. It is important to determine what makes you do your best work!

Ask yourself these questions:
Am I more productive in the morning or afternoon? When do I have the most energy? When am I able to concentrate better? Does music help me relax or break my concentration? Does dim task lighting help me stay calm and focused or do I need bright overhead light to work more productively? Would I rather hand write information or type it?

There are no right or wrong answers to these questions. You simply need to determine what works best for you and then schedule your tasks according to your preferences.

Assess when you are at your peak and tackle your most important tasks at that time. All too often people start with the easiest or quickest tasks and waste valuable time when they could be focusing on the most important tasks. Tackle the high priorities on your To Do List when you are feeling energized and watch your productivity soar!

Organize Your Work Day

Organizing your workday <u>every day</u> is another important routine that will help you on the road to time management success. Knowing what you will do each day will increase your productivity and effectiveness. Below are the steps to take to organize your workday.

- Create a schedule that reflects your priorities and goals.
- Plan the major portion of your day leaving time for interruptions or issues that may arise.
- Attack the most important projects when your energy level is high.
- Review your To Do list and meeting schedule for the day.
- Wrap up and prepare for tomorrow.

If you fail to plan, you plan to fail.

Additional Tips to Manage your Work Day

E-Mail and Phone Calls

Set up a plan for how you will handle e-mail and phone calls. Remember to be pro-active NOT reactive. You do not need to answer every phone call or every email when it is received. Build time into your schedule to check voice mail and email messages and return those that are a priority. Control your email and phone calls- do not let them control you. If not managed properly, they can reduce productivity and waste valuable time.

Meetings

It is critical to always have a set time for the start and completion of a meeting. In addition, it's important to have a clear agenda and send it to all parties that will be attending the meeting. Another thing to remember is  to be sure all the people required to make decision(s) are invited to the meeting. Many companies waste time and money on ineffective meetings. If you schedule a meeting, you are charged with the responsibility of making sure all these criteria are met.

Interruptions

It is not a matter of if, but when. No matter what job you have, you are bound to get interruptions. It could be a phone call, a visit from your boss or a co-workers that stops by to borrow something. It is important to plan for interruptions and build time into your schedule so you can adjust when they occur. When scheduling meetings, leave time to go from one to the next or chat with a co-worker who is working on a project with you. When you build time in your schedule to manage interruptions or distractions, your day will be less stressful.

Completing paperwork and filing
Schedule time in your day - everyday to process necessary paperwork and to file away things you have completed. This is a must to stay on track, manage your time effectively and avoid clutter.

Maintain an organized work space
This is another important daily task. Schedule a few minutes every day to maintain your workspace. Put things away as you are done with them and be sure your desk is cleared off at the end of each day.

Review your schedule and To Do list during the day
Periodically during the day review your Daily Planner and make adjustment where necessary. Do some of your To Do items need to be moved to tomorrow? Did one of your meetings run over time? Make notes and adjustments to help you plan ahead for the next work day.

Plan ahead for tomorrow
Use the last 15 minutes of every workday to plan for the next. This is another critical time management tool to help start your day on the right track. Plan ahead and you'll be more productive and feel more in control. When you know what to expect, it keeps stress at bay.

Have a positive attitude
It is important to feel a sense of success and accomplishment during a portion of every workday. I know it's unrealistic to think that you can have that feeling all day, everyday. But it is possible and necessary to have  that "I did it" excitement at some point in your workday. Many people ignore the positive things that happen at work and focus exclusively on the negative. If you fall into this category- make a change and fast! We spend a majority of our waking hours at work. You might as well make it enjoyable and find some good in every day. Sometimes all it takes is a change in attitude. If necessary, tweak your systems and routines until you are able to experience the feeling of some success. Without it, you are simply going through the motions. What fun is that?

Organizing for Your Office Move

Whether you are moving from one office to the next or your company is moving clear across town, planning ahead will save time, energy and money. Here are some steps to help organize your office move.

DeClutter FIRST

When decluttering and sorting, consider storage space in the new location (equal, less or more) as compared to your current space. This will help make decisions on what can be tossed and what needs to be moved.

Important Process

Be certain to schedule 15-30 minutes per day to manage this step. Tackle one area or drawer at a time.

Don't procrastinate! Start today.

What NOT to move

- Items that are no longer needed. Check your organization's retention schedules.
- Anything that can be recreated easily from a co-worker or the internet

Packing

Each employee should be responsible for packing their own belongings from their workspace.

Tips

1. Separate breakable from non-breakable items.
2. Pack boxes lightly. Keep in mind, you will need to do some lifting while unpacking.
3. Pack like things together: files, office supplies, personal items, etc.

4. Books can be very heavy. Use a smaller box and place paper between each book to avoid sticking.
5. Pack heavier items on the bottom of the box and lighter items on top.

Labeling
Box should be labeled on 4 sides: top, front and each side with the following information –
1. Employee name
2. Box number
3. Fragile (if applicable)
4. Open First (these boxes should contain business critical items that you will need immediately at the new office)

Create a Moving Inventory List
List each box and the approximate contents.

Unpacking
• Check your boxes against your inventory list.
• Unpack your "Open First" boxes.
• Organize as you unpack, box by box.

What To Do With ALL the Extra "Stuff?"
Remember, you can save a lot of money by decluttering first! I helped one busy corporation with their move and suggested they have a garage sale rather than simply disposing of all their unnecessary items. At the end of the sale, we ended up raising 50% of the cost of their move! Here's what they had to say:

"When I was first asked to lead the United Way moving process, the building filled with more than 30 years of paperwork, materials, furniture, and miscellaneous items looked like Mount Everest to me. No one knew where to start. Thankfully, Deb was able to assess our building and help us make a plan of action. She went through every office space and closet helping us to determine what to keep, what to sell, and what to toss. She spent hours actually digging through the mess right along side us. Once we determined what we were taking with us to the new building and what we were tossing, Deb helped us to organize and structure a community-wide garage sale. With her help, we

were able to cover more than half the cost of the moving service... more than $2,500! From a mess the size of Mount Everest to a more manageable move, Deb was there every step of the way. I don't know what we would have done without her. She was a lifesaver!"

Lucille H.
Office Manager and Executive
Administrative Assistant, United Way

Whether you're decluttering your workspace, increasing productivity and efficiency through time management, or streamlining a move, I hope I've been able to help you get motivated to make some important changes at work. Remember, small changes over time yield big results!

CHAPTER 7

Creating Work-Life Balance

What is work-life balance? Wikipedia, the web based free encyclopedia defines work-life balance as "a concept including proper prioritizing between "work" (career and ambition) on one hand and "lifestyle" (health, pleasure, leisure, family and spiritual development/mediation) on the other hand." Simply speaking, it is the balance you create between your work and home life. Where do you stand? Take the quiz on the next page and find out. It's important to know where you are so you can determine where you need to go.

Work-Life Balance Quiz
Answer True or False

1. Most days every minute is scheduled regardless of how much I try to slow down. T F

2. I feel like I don't have any time for my family, friends or myself. T F

3. Sometimes I wish I had a different job or career. T F

4. I cannot remember the last time I took a day off and did something for myself. T F

5. I don't know the last time I read a book for pleasure. T F

6. I feel stressed out most of the time. T F

7. Sometimes I do not use all my vacation days from work. T F

8. More often than not, I feel exhausted, even early in the work-week. T F

9. Sometimes I miss family events or spending time with friends because I am working. T F

10. Frequently I bring home work from the office. T F

11. My family complains I am working too much. T F

12. I dread going to work everyday. T F

Scoring: Give yourself 1 point for every True answer

0-2 – Good for you! You have created excellent work-life balance. Keep it up!

3-5 – Things are starting to feel overwhelming! Begin to make changes now to get back on track.

6 or more – Your life is in a state of chaos. Take action immediately before it begins to take a toll on your health!

So, how did you do? If you did not fair well, you are not alone. With the boom in technology, it is easier for people to stay connected to their work 24 hours a day, 7 days a week through email and voice mail. The ability to be connected to our work even when we are "off duty" has gotten completely out of control. It affects our family life and our health. The average 40 hour work week for many is non-existant. To keep up at the office, employees are working longer hours. This has forced a decrease in the time available for family and pleasure in addition to causing a significant amount of stress.

According to the National Institute for Occupational Safety and Health in Cincinnati, Ohio, studies show that *"the workplace has become the single greatest source of stress"*. The problems caused by stress have become a concern for employees and employers. The number of stress related disability claims has doubled in recent years according to the Employee Assistance Professionals Association in Arlington, Virginia. Stress in and of itself can cause a variety of other health issues.

Many employers are now acknowledging the importance of work-life balance for their employees and are taking steps to support the changes necessary for it to occur. As an individual there are many changes that you can make today to move toward more balance in your life.

Here are some of my tips for creating work-life balance:

1 - Make a commitment to schedule personal time at least one hour every week to do something you enjoy.

2 - Cultivate new friendships or reconnect with someone you may have lost touch with because life became "too busy".

3 - Clear your schedule of activities that are non-productive or not enjoyable.

4 - Schedule time everyday to exercise- even if it is for only 15 minutes. Start small and build in additional time as often as you can.

5 - DeClutter Your Home. Make your home your sanctuary, many people work more to avoid being in a cluttered home.

6 - At the end of each day, find something to be grateful for and add it to a journal.

7 - Set priorities. What are the top five things I want to accomplish for the week, month and year?

8 - Eat healthier. Add more fruits and vegetables to your diet and decrease/limit unhealthy foods.

9 - Read or listen to music more often. These are calming activities that can help reduce stress.

10- Try to go to bed the same time every night. Getting a good night's sleep is critical to stress reduction.

11- Limit the time you spend on work related tasks when you are at home.

12- Turn off your cell phone or put the ringer on vibrate at least 1-2 nights per week.

13- Don't feel guilty. It is ok to spend time enjoying yourself or relaxing. Rest will help you rejuvenate.

14- When you are not working, try not to think about work.

15- Volunteer or do something for a family member, friend or neighbor.

16- Stop trying to do it all. Share household responsibilities with family members.

17- Create a morning routine that is more peaceful and less hurried.

18- Avoid electronic and internet overload. Is it adding or detracting from the quality of your life?

19- Have a sense of humor. Being serious all the time is no fun! Inject humor and laughter into everyday.

20- Don't over-schedule yourself or your family. Keep a family calendar.

21- Eat dinner together as a family (with no TV on!) as often as possible. This will give you time to connect and enjoy each other's company.

22- Try not to bring work stress home with you.

23- Be flexible and deal with issues as they arise. Remember, nothing is ever set in stone or forever.

24- Don't sweat the small stuff. Stay calm and count to 10. When we are stressed the little things look so much bigger than they really are, don't they?

25- Dream big. It's ok to have a dream and work hard to accomplish it. No dream is too crazy if it is something you are truly passionate about.

Now that you have some ideas, you're probably saying to yourself, where do I begin? Find a nice comfy place to curl up with some paper and a pen and ask yourself these questions:

What would my perfect life look like?
What would I be doing?
What goals do I want to accomplish?

What can I do to take steps to achieve them?
Who will be supporting me in these goals?
What are my limitations?
What is stopping me from moving forward?

I know this is a lot to think about. The key is that you need to begin thinking about it! Then, you need to start writing it down. As we discussed in the previous chapter, you are more likely to achieve the balance you are looking for in your life if you write down your goals and dreams.

Here's a challenge. I call it Two for Today! What two things will you do for yourself today (and every day going forward) to help move toward one or more of your goals and dreams and create work-life balance? Think about what they might be. Maybe you will go for a walk or read a chapter or two in a book or reach out and call a friend. The choice is yours. Make the choice and just do it. Two things every day! Write them down in your calendar or planner. Make a commitment and don't let yourself down.

Two for Today!

1. _____

2. _____

It is important to remember that it is impossible to have work-life balance all the time. There are certain times where work will need to take a priority (for example an accountant during tax season.) What we are shooting for is balance most of the time. A life that is enjoyable, rewarding and less stressed.

In order to create change you must do things differently than you are doing them today. Change is never easy, but the rewards are almost always filled with unexpected surprises. Creating work-life balance is extremely important. You deserve it! Now go make it happen!

CHAPTER 8

Maintaining a Clutter-Free Life – You Can Do It!

Congratulations, you made it! I knew you could!

If you've come this far, you deserve a big pat on the back! By now you're probably feeling great -- whether you've met your goals for organizing your home, your workspace, or your life, or you're well on your way there, the most important part is to now maintain.

When I work with clients, I don't just show them how to organize, I teach them the methods and systems they can use to keep their lives in order, for good!

Maintaining Your Systems

The most important part of maintaining is figuring out what works best for you. I can't tell you how to best maintain what you've created - only you can decide that for yourself!

Some people like to spend a set time, such as ten minutes each day to work on maintaining the clutter in their homes, offices, or lives. For others, it might be too much to spend time each day. Some of my clients take an hour every Saturday morning to catch up on decluttering and ensure that they don't fall back into the same old routines.

What works for me may not work for you, and what works for you is different than what works for someone else. The most important thing is to set up a plan for maintenance, establish routines, and stick to them at all costs!

Remember: it takes 21 days to create a new habit. Be persistent and don't quit!

Easier said than done, right?

Let's get excited about all the hard work you have done! All your plans and routines are in place to organize you home, your workspace and your life. As hard as you worked to set them up, in order to make them last, you will need to be diligent. You'll need to take it one step further. You'll need to make these new systems and routines become new habits.

The Difference Between a Routine and a Habit

Let's talk a bit about routines. They are things we do everyday like shower, brush our teeth and or some have a cup of coffee in the morning. We eat three meals a day and go to bed every night. Routines are automatic. It is almost like you can do them without really thinking. Apparently, according to the research... you are! Routines are created over time because they are done repetitively and consistently. After a certain amount of time (21 days) the routines become a habit. Once a habit, the chances of falling back into your old patterns are much less likely.

So if you are working on changing old routines like throwing your clothes on the floor rather than hanging them up or keeping things in your head instead of writing them down, your current habits will try to stop you in your tracks. So for the next 21 days, until the

21 days to form a habit!

new routines becomes habits, you will need to work very hard to forge ahead. Are you up for the challenge? Of course you are! The best way to tackle any new routine is to break it down into bite size pieces. Try to implement one or two new routines at a time for 3-4 days. Most people can do anything for that amount of time, can't they? Anyone that has dieted before knows that.

At the end of the four days, think long and hard about the new changes you've implemented. Even if you are not convinced that you can stick to it, make a commitment to yourself that you will continue the new routines or behaviors for another week. Now you are at 10 or 11 days. You're half way there, why quit now?

By this time, hopefully you are starting to become a believer. Things should be falling into place. Now you are getting excited and thinking of a few more routines you can implement. The 21 days are over and you've done it! Congratulations! It may have been harder than you thought, but doesn't it feel good to accomplish something you did not think you could do?

Remember, it is important to implement a few changes at a time. It would be too much to expect yourself to make more than that at one time. You are looking for new life long skills to get you where you want to be. Invest the energy and tackle things in due time. Slow and steady wins the race!

Three Important Steps to Maintaining

<u>1 - Create new routines that will become habits!</u>

For many people, clutter is a result of long-held bad habits. As you've learned in this book, it's all about changing your current routines and creating new ones that will work for you.

If shopping is a source of constant clutter accumulation, here are some ideas to help you break the habit and try something new!

10 clutter-busting things to do instead of going shopping:
1. Weed out catalogues and magazines.
2. Make a scrapbook with your children's photos or
     photos from a vacation.

3. Update your address book.
4. Organize your kitchen junk drawer.
5. Throw out expired coupons.
6. Organize and label old photos.
7. Spend one hour getting rid of clutter in the basement, garage or attic.
8. Roll loose change.
9. Throw away old makeup and toiletries.
10. Organize wrapping paper, gift bags, bows, etc.

2- Have an Accountability Buddy!

My number one mission is to motivate and inspire people to achieve their decluttering and time management goals! I would love to be there, cheering you on, all the time, but I can't! So enlist the help of someone close to you for support and encouragement. When you have an accountability buddy who you know is rooting for you, but ready to remind you when you need reminding, you'll be more likely to stay on track. It's got to be somebody that you know is going to hold your feet to the fire. Offer to do the same for them.

3 - Stay positive and don't give up!

Remember the song, "Mama said they'll be days like this"? Well, there will be days where you will want to just quit because it seems impossible to change your life. Expect them and you'll be more prepared to handle them.

Everyone who has made life changes whether they were to lose weight, quit smoking or get out of debt, all faced obstacles to completing their goal. It's ok! You may have a bad day or two or three. What's important is to get right back on track

and continue the course. Keep telling yourself that YOU CAN do this and you will!

Final Thoughts on Maintaining

Life is constantly evolving. Families change, kids change, jobs change, and as they do, the clutter in your house and the clutter in your life will change, too! The issues and challenges you face now will be different from the ones you face five years, five months, and sometimes even five minutes from now. At the beginning of this book, I promised to show you ways to help you declutter and organize your life -- and stay that way. Now I'll make you another promise: life will always change!

In order to stay on track, you must remember the fact that the one thing you can be certain of in life is change. Maintaining your organizational systems, whether they're for home, work, or your life, is all about being flexible and rolling with those changes. Nothing, no matter how large or small, is set in stone. Ever.

Because life is always changing and evolving, the best thing to do is to just roll with the changes. Is that difficult? Sure, sometimes! But in order to maintain, you must know that it will take a conscious effort on your part to tweak and alter the systems you've set up so that they work for you and your family. Be flexible! Be willing to shift gears! Do this and you won't be disappointed.

Maintaining an organized, simplified life takes work, but the benefits are endless. I'm cheering for you! You can do this! Happy organizing!

Still Looking for Some "Organization Motivation"? We've Got You Covered!

Log onto The DeClutter Coach website, decluttercoachdeb.com, to find out more about our residential organizing services!

www.DeClutterCoachDeb.com

For corporate clients, visit DC Efficiency Consulting

www.DCeffconsult.com

Or, check out our television show:

www.organizationmotivation.com

To find out more about our news segments:

www.organizedin60seconds.com

Like us on Facebook to get daily doses of inspiration, and let us know how you're doing. You can also follow us on Twitter, and connect with us on Linked In!

- www.facebook.com/decluttercoachdeb
- www.twitter.com/deborahjcabral
- www.linkedin.com/in/deborahjcabral

The DeClutter Coach team would love to hear from you!

The DeClutter Coach's
5 Steps to Organizing Anything!

C lear the area to be organized. Set up a staging area for sorting.

O pen the trash. Toss broken items. Set up 2 boxes: one for items to donate/sell and one for items that belong in another room/space.

A rrange like things together (only those items remaining in the space)

C ompartmentalize, containerize. Put things back into the space in an orderly fashion. Use clear bins, labels, etc. Use all of the vertical space. Create a system that will work for you.

H ave a maintenance plan.